Lattice Braceletts
Beadwork
Book I

by
C J David

Cover Photo by Vallerie David

Cover design and photograph by Vallerie David
Illustrations by C J David

Printed in the United States of America

Published by American Supply Company Publishing
Cave Junction, Oregon

First Printing November 1996

ISBN 0-9655049-0-5
Library of Congress Catalogue Card Number 96-95043

Table of Contents

Introduction

Hello out there! Welcome beadworkers, to yet another expression of your art.

The beauty of the lattice technique by using two needles on each end of one thread is the ability to create a balanced design without the use of a loom. While BEADS ARE BEAUTIFUL, our unique projects also create soft, tactile "nice to the touch" and oh, so pretty bracelets!

Examples are given with suggested color combinations, however it is expected that your individual creativity will lead you to wonderful selections of your own.

Enjoy! Enjoy! Enjoy!

CJD

Acknowledgments

The journey into the realm of instructive writing could not have been accomplished without the encouragement of my family. Their help has sustained me. My thanks to my daughter, Kristen for her patient hours in assembling of data and especially her computer literacy. And my gratitude to my son, Charles, who not only is proficient with the computer but has displayed an extraordinary aptitude for design, as has his wife Vallerie, in showing such expertise by her photography on the cover.

My appreciation goes out as well to those bead shops that have dazzled my eyes with their smorgasbord of materials, tempted my pocketbook and inspired my creative side.

Among those shops, who could only be described as mind boggling in their vast selections (as well as moderate in their pricing), I would like to first name Fire Mountain Gems. From my own home town, they have provided for me, along with thousands of other beadworkers and jewelry makers nationwide, an exceptional array of supplies. Their newest line of seed beads will contribute greatly to any color selection.

Also in Oregon, I have utilized the immense offering of beads from the Baker Bay Bead Company. Their store is a heaven on earth for the person who enjoys seeing wall to wall color in a seemingly endless rainbow of beaded hanks. Their selection is truly wonderful!!

And I could not go without mentioning my favorite shop in Laguna Beach. The continuing ambience of The Bead Shop, from which I accumulated my first collection of beads, draws me again and again as one of the highlights of my visits to Southern California. Their layout and displays, attended by a very helpful staff, contain some of the most unique selections for assembly of original designs.

Addresses for these suppliers may be found at the back page.

With the knowledge and appreciation I feel for those people and places, I look forward to making the acquaintance of many more.

CJD

About the Author

C.J. David owns & runs Siskiyou Vineyards winery in Southern Oregon. When she is not working in the fields or making sales across Oregon, she can usually be found on her ranch working on one of her many crafty hobbies. She loves to immerse herself in her latest projects, and her fingers never have a still moment.

Besides running a business for the last 22 years, she has raised her two children, Kristen and Charles. Always on the go C. J. learns new tips and shares her talents & ideas with others. No matter where she is, it seems she has onlookers wondering what she is working on. Ever the teacher, she explains with dedication each craft and its technique.

Materials

Beads: Size 11 seed beads
     (Size 10 seed beads may be used, but will create a larger size of work.)

Needles: Size 12 or 13 bead needles. Length is not critical, but a needle that will reliably pass through all beads (many times twice through) is a must. Often available in packages of 25, only three needles will be used for these projects.

Thread: Size O for #11 beads. The larger the bead a correspondingly larger thread can be used.

Thread for cord ties: The equivalent of 12, 12" pieces of 6 strand embroidery floss in colors blending with chosen beads.

Wax: Beeswax or paraffin (Candle wax will do).

Scissors: Small with sharp blades and good point.

CAUTION! ! Beadwork can be habit forming!!

About the Procedures

The Lattice design is unique. It produces a balanced design, exactly the same on both sides. By using <u>two</u> needles working back and forth as seen in the illustrations, each side will be even; allowing for concentration on design.

Do refer to NOTES found at the end of instructions since some hints and recommendations are repeated for different projects and pattern. Before commencing your first project, take a close look at the diagrams to understand the concept of "where you are going" from the starting point.

I suggest you start with Bracelet "A" as it is a simpler form of this beading. You will notice then, that the pattern will be substantially altered visually by the simple use of color change (as evidenced in Bracelet A-1, 2, and 3).Each pattern for bracelets is given with three alternative color combinations resulting in different projects.

On the subject of color, it should be noted that with glass beads, there is not only a vast selection in hue, but also a choice as to whether that color is opaque, transparent, flat (matte finish), metallic, or brightly faceted. When placed side by side or in groups, the colors react and play against one another in often surprising ways. I find as an alternative to merely gathering three, four, or five colors that really look pretty together, is to proceed to work them into some kind of pattern. Then, and only then can I <u>really</u> see how well these beads successfully combine.

It is also possible to somewhat match your working thread with your selected colors, making it less visible. I tend to confine my selection to black or white.

A word on waxing your thread. I tend to pull my thread through the wax about 3 or 4 times. Careful! Thread seems to "jump" while being pulled and should be checked to see that knots have not occurred. Beyond strengthening and protecting your thread, this waxing comes in especially handy when threading a needle. A sturdy point can be created on the thread end. Squeeze this point between the thumb and forefinger, sliding it immediately through the eye of the needle. Beading needles are TINY. . . so be patient!

By following the patterns in Bracelets "A" through "K" you may be encouraged to venture on in creating patterns and color combinations of your own. Blank graphs can be found at the back of the book for your use in copying and planning your own designs.

Important: Diagrams are drawn for simplicity in viewing the beading procedure. Whether you are left or right handed, your work can be held either as the diagram is seen, or your work can (and should) be turned around to work back on the next row. This of course means the diagram would be read in reverse for that row.

Bracelet "A-1"

Color Code: (A) Transparent dark green
                       (B) Transparent gold
                       (C) Opaque green
                       (D) Matte yellow

Wax approximately 3 feet of thread.
Thread 2 needles, one at each end.

Step 1)   Begin with 2(A), 1(B), 2(A), 1(B), 4(A), 2(B).

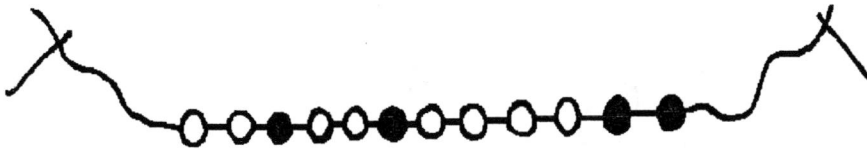

Step 2)   Circle around to pick up the last single colored bead.

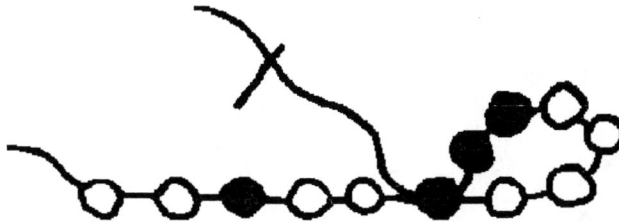

At this point, leave the end of one thread longer than the other so that further on, thread can be added at different places.

Step 3)   Add 3(B), pick up second single color.

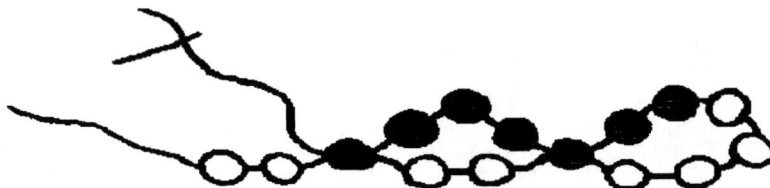

Step 4)   Add 2(B). Leave this needle.

Step 5)   Pick up the second needle. Add 2(A), go through last bead on other thread.

From this point and throughout your work, pull beads together firmly from time to time.

Step 6)   Add 2(B), 1(C) and join to second row. See NOTE A.

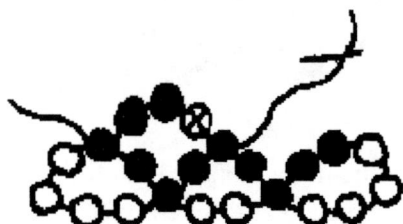

Step 7)   Add 1(C), 2(B) and join to second row. See NOTE B.

Step 8)   Turning into the fourth row, add 2(A), 2(B). Join to third row.

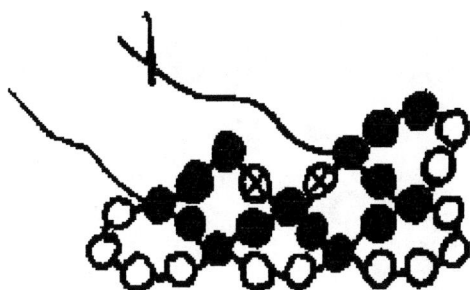

Step 9)   Add 1(C), 1(D), 1(C). Join to third row.

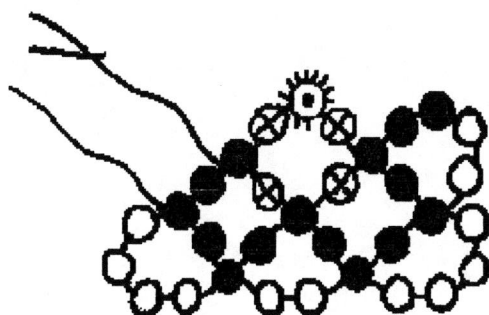

Step 10)   Add 2(B). Leave this needle.

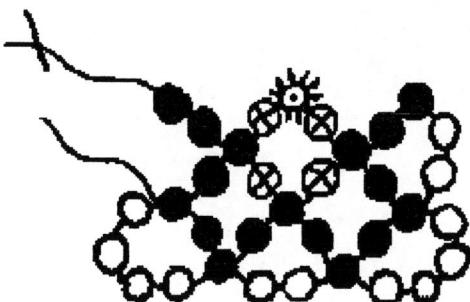

Step 11)   Pick up the first needle. Add 2(A). Go through the last bead on the other thread.

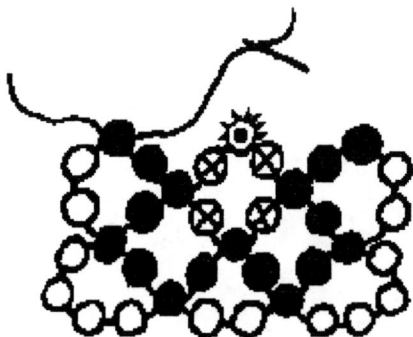

Step 12)   Repeat steps 6-11 until desired length. See NOTES C and D.

Step 13)   Add 3(B).

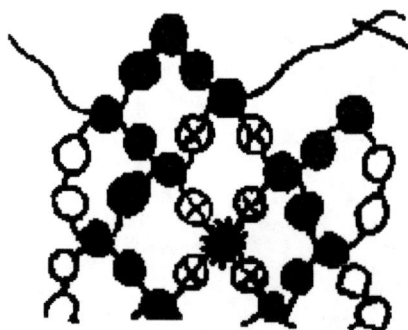

Step 14)   Add 3(B).

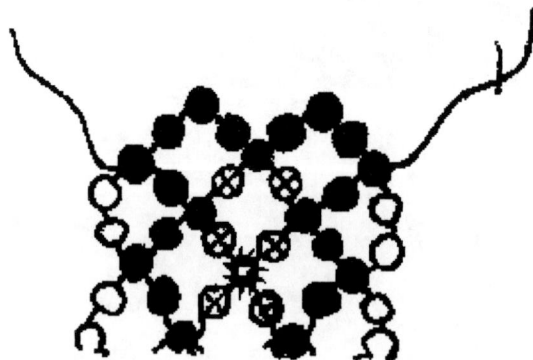

Step 15)   Add 4(A).

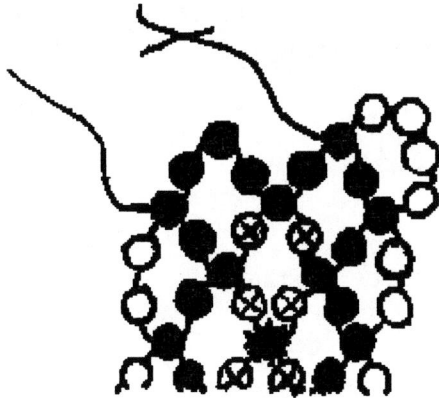

Step 16)   Add 2(A).

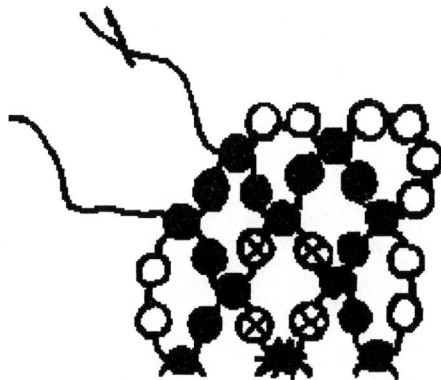

Step 17)   Add 4(A).

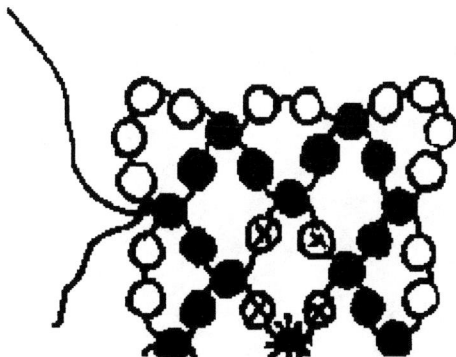

Tighten thread and tie together into a square knot. To hide ends, work thread back through about 12 to 15 beads and cut ends carefully close to work. Route each thread through a different path following an already worked thread.

NOTES - Helpful Hints

A) The first two rows will often twist while adding the third row. Simply turn beads around to their correct position, as indicated on the illustration.

B) Here, either thread can be worked next. However, you can always tell which side was worked last, because the last three beads worked can easily be pulled loose. I usually continue working on that thread.

C) The length of each bracelet is determined by two things:
1) The size of the wearer's wrist, and
2) The pattern. Example

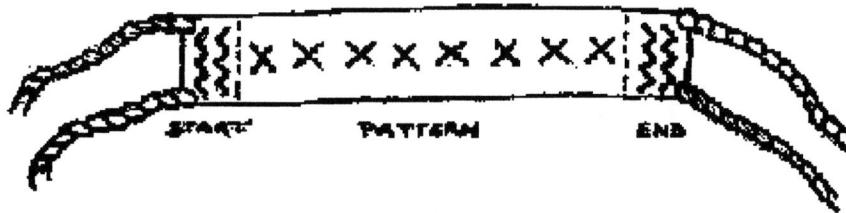

Always leave enough working space to end your pattern in a mirror image of the way you started it. The entire length of the bracelet, finished, should be about 3/4" to 1" shorter than the wrist. This allows space for tying corded ends.

D) Check to see that your pattern is ended the same way it was begun. To do this, fold your work as illustrated to compare the layout of beads.

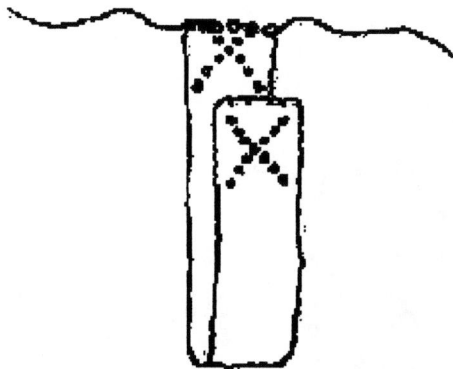

Adding New Thread

It is expected that at some point the first of your two thread ends will become too short. (Remember - at the start, in Step 2 we made certain that one thread end would be longer than the other.)When your working thread is down to about 4 inches (don't let it get too short to be easily manipulated) leaving the needle on that thread, lay aside your work to follow this procedure:

Step 1   Thread a 20 " to 24" waxed thread with one needle , having it ready to use.

Step 2   Now, pick up your work and start the first beads into a new row.

Leave this thread

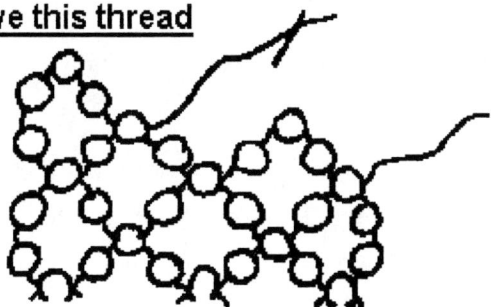

Step 3   Using the newly threaded needle, pick up the next 3 beads in the pattern. If you need to, you may use a small piece of tape on the thread to prevent beads from falling from the end while you continue the row to the end. Leave a 4 or 5 inch tail; enough to easily tie a knot.

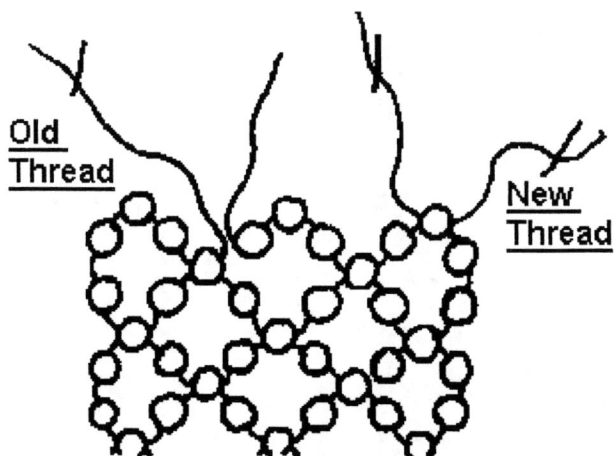

Old Thread

New Thread

Step 4   Pulling up your threads so there will be no spaces between the beads, carefully tie the old end and the new tail into a **square** knot. (Right over left - pull tight, and left over right - pull tight.)

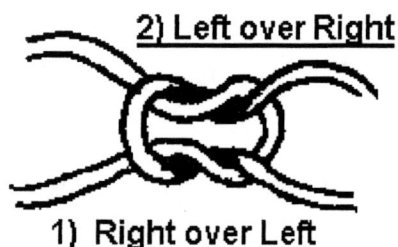

2) Left over Right

1) Right over Left

Remember, beading thread is so small, you won't be able to see if the knot is correct, so get it **right**!

Step 5   Ready to weave in the first tail. Using the thread with the needle, thread through beads, working over already completed work. Check reverse side to be sure your needle is going through the beads.

Step 6   When you have woven through 12 to 15 beads, thread should be securely hidden. Clip thread close to beadwork. After enough beading has been completed further on the work, thread the remaining end on a needle and work into beads in the reverse direction of the other end thread.

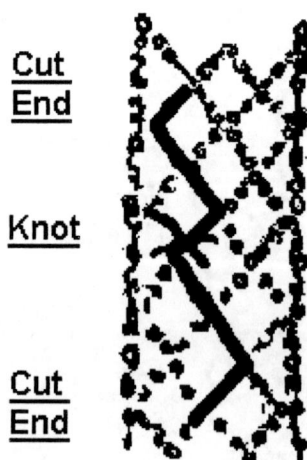

Cut
End

Knot

Cut
End

A Word About Cordage

Cordage, as the system of taking fibers, twisting them by hand, and creating a rope, cord, or string, is one of the oldest pursuits of ancient peoples.

Originally, (and I address the days before DMC, et al), the fibers were taken from plants, trees, and often the sinew of animals. Cordage can be made as fine as sewing thread, or as coarse and large as marine rope. I have used Dogbane, Milkweed, Nettle, Evening Primrose, Wild Grape, Cotton, Flax, Cedar fibers, and Sinew. The method of extending the length is only slightly different than the following diagrams.

In short, cordage is more than simply twisting some threads. It is an exciting adventure into nature and ancient cultural activity.

Tie Cord For Bracelet

Many of us with handwork as a hobby or even profession find ourselves with an abundance of 'left-over' embroidery thread. The cording described here is a great way to make use of these odds and ends if you have them.

As with the beads themselves, the variety of embroidery thread colors is endless. And don't forget the metallics! A matched color cord can be enhanced with a gold or silver highlight. Blending threads to match your work is great fun and completes your work with a professional customization.

Step 1 Select 2, 3, 4, or 5 (even 6 if your wish) colors of 6 strand embroidery thread to match the beadwork. Decide which colors may need <u>more</u> strands than others to blend together to achieve a similar balance of color in the bracelet.

Step 2 Cut the selected colors into 12 inch lengths. At this point it is possible to twist lengths together in several combinations to compare and visualize the end result and how it will look on the bracelet.

Step 3 Use 18 to 22 strands <u>total</u> for twisting the cord. These may be in combinations of any number of each color. For example, I often take a 6 strand length and divide it in two, three strand pieces. I also use two strands of one color for a less dominant color in the bracelet. Mix and twist the chosen threads for a final decision in matching the bracelet. When your final selection of colors is made, lay out four piles of the same color combinations.

Step 4 Using a thread or crochet hook, pull the first pile of threads as selected above, through the corner beads of the bracelet.

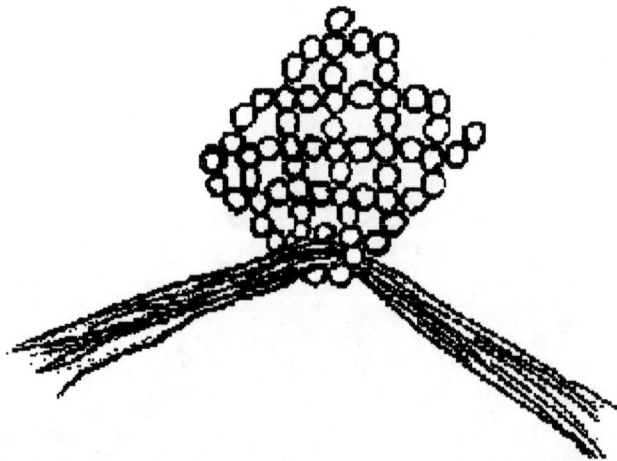

Step 5 Place the beadwork directly in the middle of the threads and commence to twist the threads together, twisting one way with the left hand and the other way with the right.

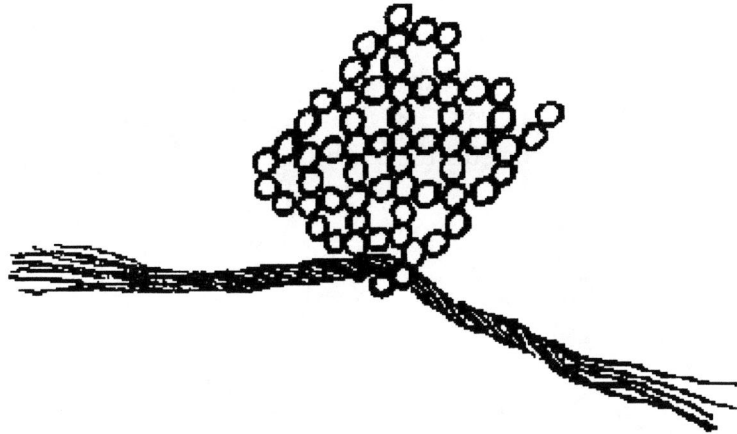

Step 6 Holding the <u>tightly</u> twisted portion of the threads together with one hand, take the beadwork in the other hand and (keeping its position in the middle of the threads) allow the bracelet to turn with the twist, into a CORD!

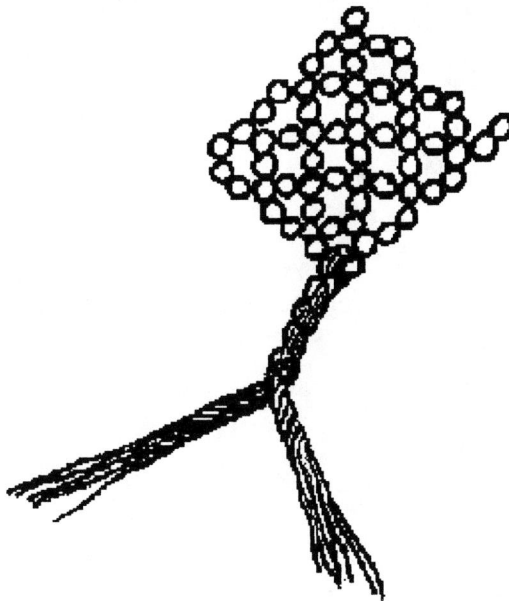

Step 7 Continue twisting both sides of the threads evenly while allowing the bracelet to turn as it twists into the cord.

<u>Step 8</u>   Twist to the end of the threads and complete with an overhand knot. I
             leave a length of about 3/8 of an inch, trimming the threads to resemble a
             tassel. This completes the cord.

Repeat the steps 4 through 8 for each of the remaining three corners of the bracelet
        and your bracelet will be complete!
BRAVO!!

About the Design Diagrams

The following graphs will show 11 different designs each with 3 alternative color combinations, giving you 33 different projects. Each of these designs are to be worked in the same technique as described in "Directions" starting on page 11.

Once you have accustomed yourself to working your bracelets in the lattice technique, you are encouraged to make copies of the graphs provided on pages 48 - 50 to use for your own inspired designs. Don't forget, if a color combination or certain placement of color doesn't work, try it another way. But keep in mind also, that some of the strangest "starts" turn out to be some very acceptable designs. I have proceeded to work on designs I truly thought were at the least, unhandsome, only to discover that when they were completed they were exceedingly attractive. As they say. . . go figure.

In any case, have fun!

H	A-1	H-2	A-2	B-3	A-3	D-2	D-3	D-1	B-2	B	B	B-1

A				**Layout**
A-1				**of**
A				**Front Cover**
				Designs

H-3	K-1	C-1	B	G-1
				I-1
				F-1
				E-1
				J-1
				H
				H-1

Not Shown: C-2, C-3, E-2, E-3, F-2, F-3, G-2, G-3, I-2, I-3, J-2, J-3.

Note: Where letters only are shown bracelett design is illustrated, but there is no color combination listed.

A

Color Selections for Bracelet A

1.

A) ○ *Transparent dark green*
B) ⊙ *Transparent gold*
C) ⊗ *Opaque teal green*
D) ● *Matte yellow*

2.

A) ○ *Black/ white stripe*
B) ⊙ *Transparent blue*
C) ⊗ *Black*
D) ● *Matte blue-green*

3.

A) ○ *Blue/ white stripe*
B) ⊙ *Transparent blue*
C) ⊗ *White opaque*
D) ● *Matte gray*

Notes

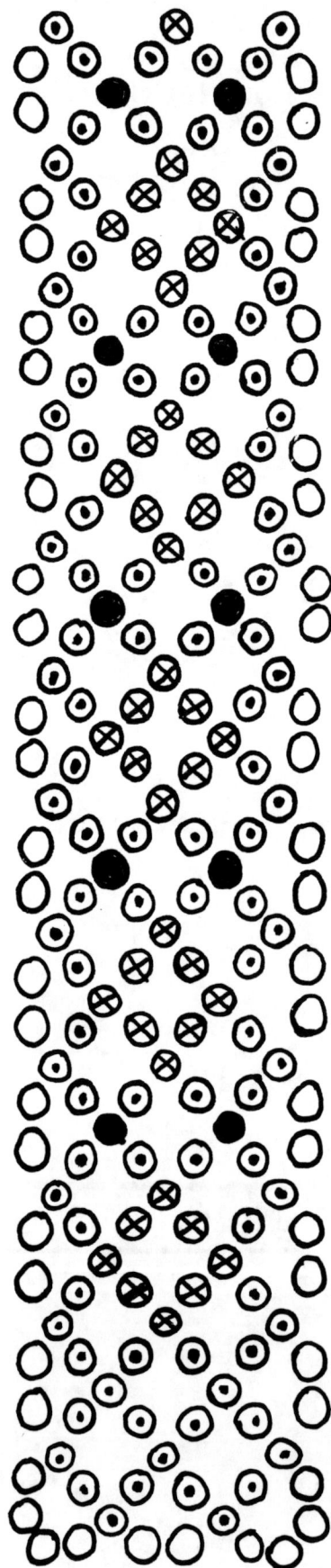

B

Color Selections for Bracelet B

1.

A) ○   *Dark metallic green*
B) ⊙   *Transparent gold*
C) ⊗   *Transparent olive green*
D) ●   *Transparent dark green*

2.

A) ○   *Opaque dark red*
B) ⊙   *Transparent pink (gold highlights)*
C) ⊗   *Transparent red (gold highlights)*
D) ●   *Pearl white*

3.

A) ○   *Transparent blue*
B) ⊙   *Black*
C) ⊗   *Metallic blue*
D) ●   *Pearl lavender*

Notes

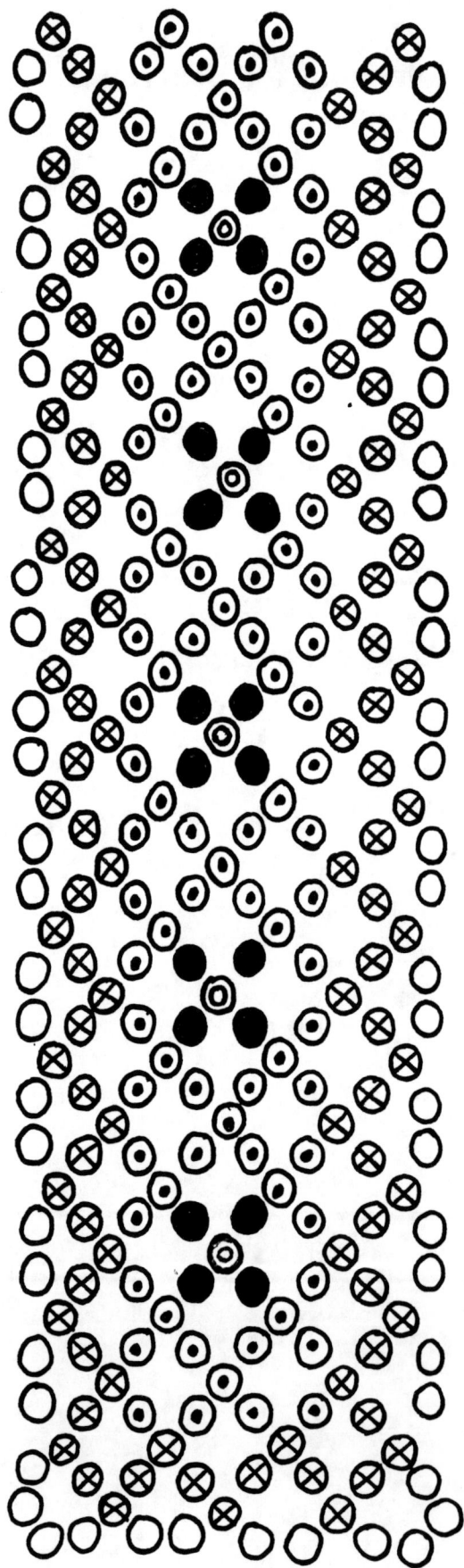

C

Color Selections for Bracelet C

1.

A) ○   *Transparent purple*
B) ⊙   *White*
C) ✪   *Light Blue*
D) ●   *Pearl lavender*
E) ◉   *Metallic black (hematite)*

2.

A) ○   *Transparent pink (gold highlights)*
B) ⊙   *Transparent brown*
C) ✪   *Pearl White*
D) ●   *Dark Red*
E) ◉   *Gold*

3.

A) ○   *Transparent yellow*
B) ⊙   *Coffee*
C) ✪   *Transparent coffee*
D) ●   *White*
E) ◉   *Yellow*

Notes

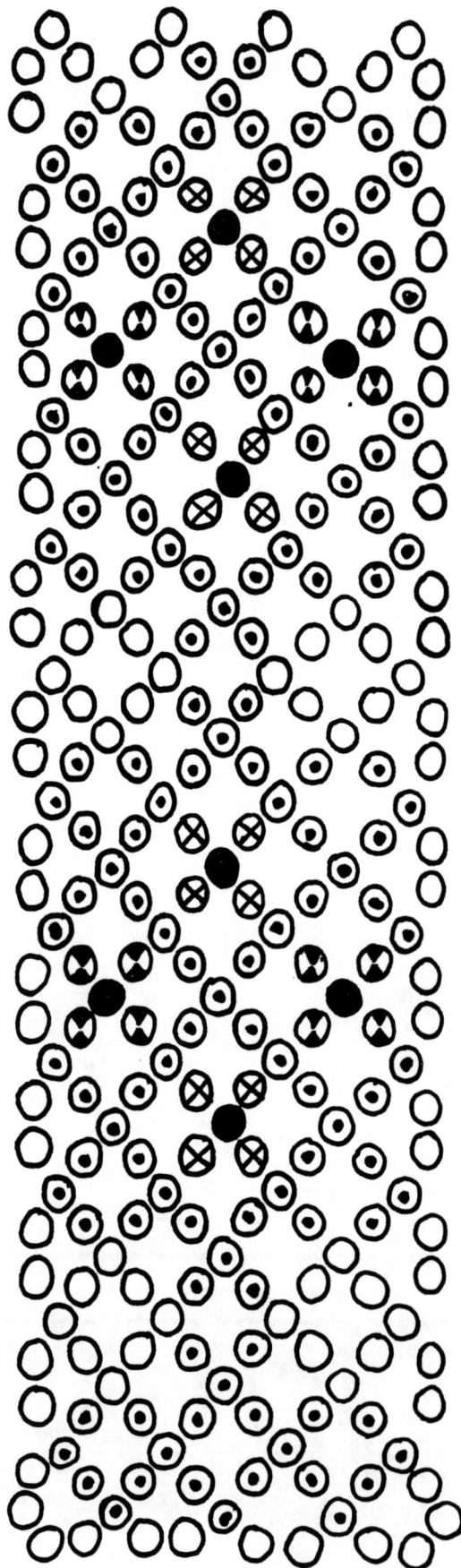

D

Color Selections for Bracelet D

1.

A)	○	*Transparent gold*
B)	⊙	*White*
C)	✪	*Transparent brown*
D)	●	*Yellow*
E)	✪	*Coffee*

2.

A)	○	*Transparent purple*
B)	⊙	*White*
C)	✪	*Dark metallic blue*
D)	●	*Light blue*
E)	✪	*Metallic black (hematite)*

3.

A)	○	*Transparent light coffee*
B)	⊙	*Dark red-brown*
C)	✪	*Silver*
D)	●	*Dark red*
E)	✪	*Pearl white*

Notes

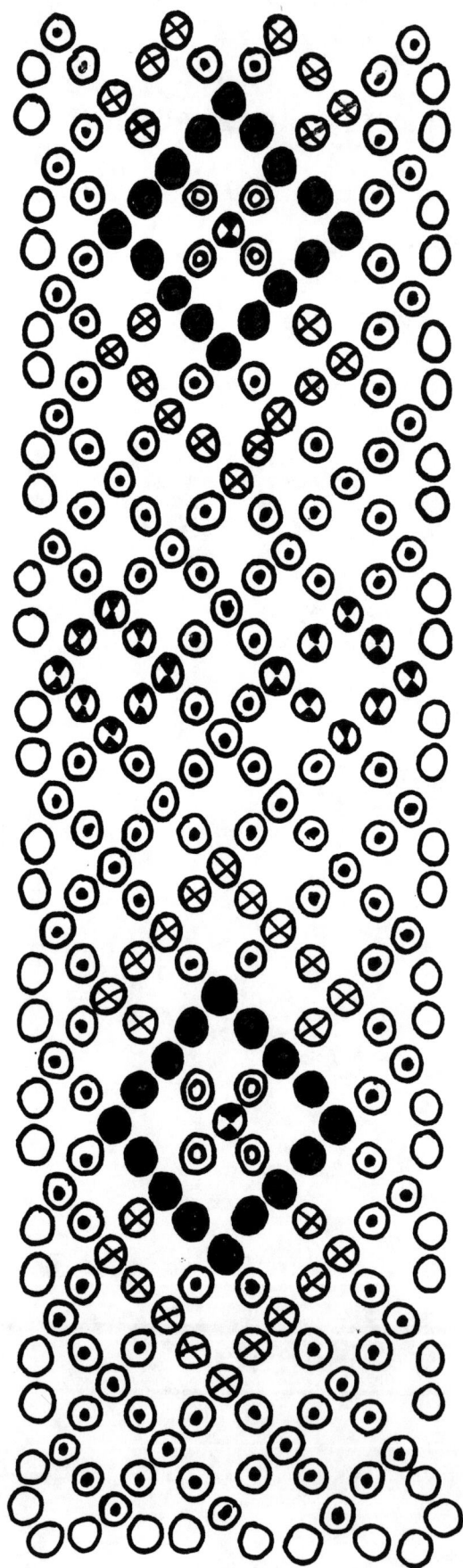

E

Color Selections for Bracelet E

1.

A) ○   *Faceted green*
B) ◉   *Pearl white*
C) ✪   *Chartreuse green*
D) ●   *Light faceted green*
E) ◎   *Dark metallic blue*
F) ✪   *Transparent blue-green*

2.

A) ○   *Dark brown*
B) ◉   *Transparent coffee*
C) ✪   *Yellow*
D) ●   *Pearl coffee*
E) ◎   *White*
F) ✪   *Transparent orange (rainbow)*

3.

A) ○   *Pearl blue*
B) ◉   *Transparent gray*
C) ✪   *Light blue-green*
D) ●   *Transparent green*
E) ◎   *Dark blue green*
F) ✪   *Dark metallic blue*

Notes

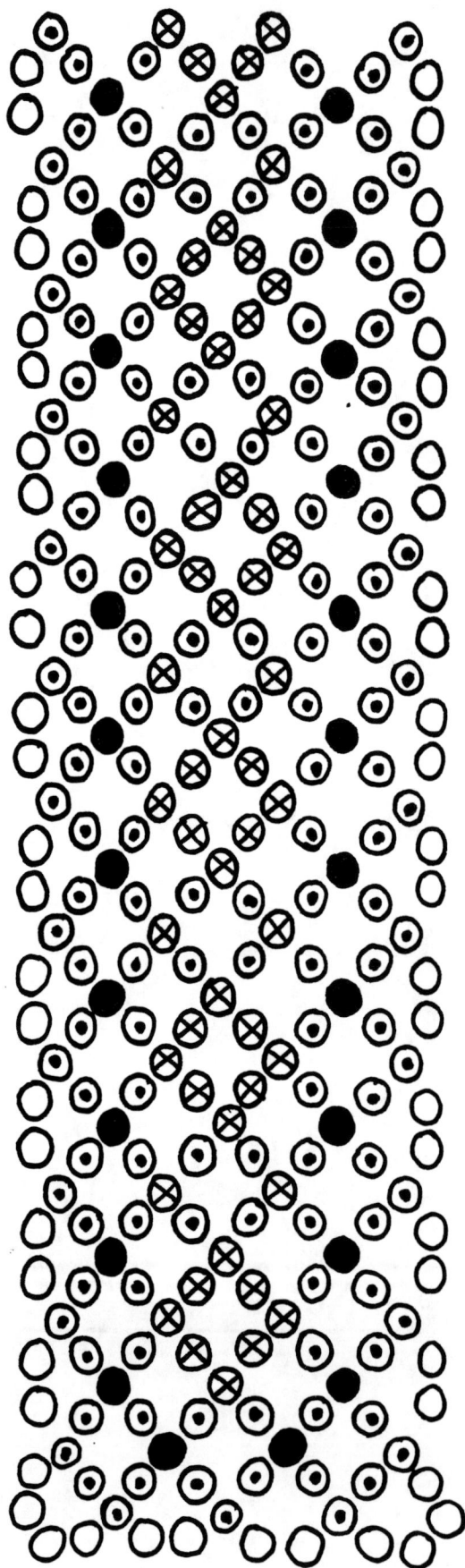

F

Color Selections for Bracelet F

1.

A) ○ *Gold*
B) ⊙ *Transparent brown*
C) ✪ *Transparent gold*
D) ● *Red*

2.

A) ○ *Transparent dark blue*
B) ⊙ *Transparent gray*
C) ✪ *Pearl blue*
D) ● *Black*

3.

A) ○ *Black*
B) ⊙ *Creamy pearl*
C) ✪ *Transparent olive green*
D) ● *Teal green*

Notes

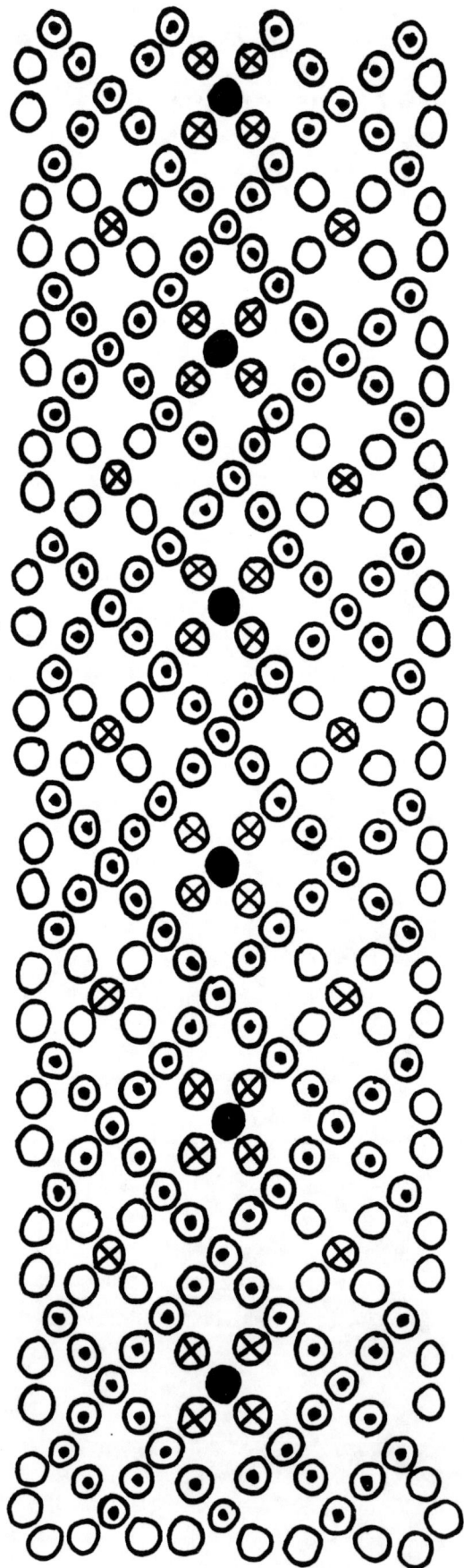

G

38

Color Selections for Bracelet G

1.

A) ○ *Matte purple*
B) ◉ *Transparent dark green*
C) ⊗ *Transparent lavender w/ blue highlights*
D) ● *Pearl white*

2.

A) ○ *Matte blue-green*
B) ◉ *Pearl white*
C) ⊗ *White*
D) ● *Turquoise*

3.

A) ○ *White*
B) ◉ *Transparent light coffee*
C) ⊗ *Yellow*
D) ● *Transparent yellow-green*

Notes

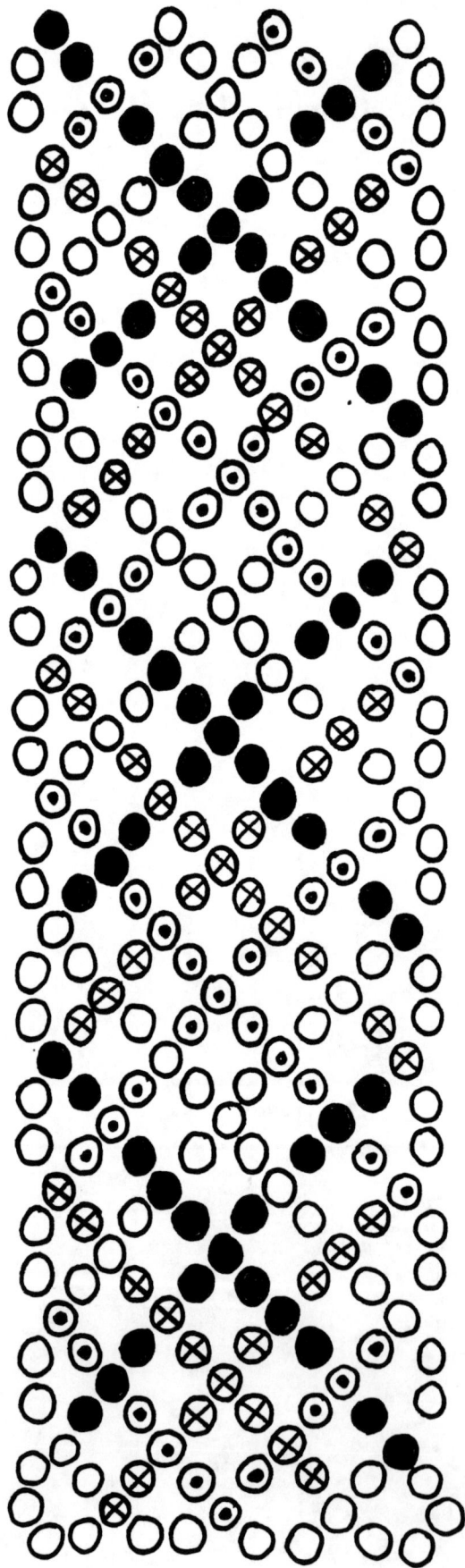

H

Color Selections for Bracelet H

1.

A) ○   *Transparent coffee*
B) ⊙   *Pearl white*
C) ⊗   *Matte yellow*
D) ●   *Yellow*

2.

A) ○   *Black metallic*
B) ⊙   *Bronze*
C) ⊗   *Silver*
D) ●   *Gold*

3.

A) ○   *Pearl coffee*
B) ⊙   *Transparent purple*
C) ⊗   *Transparent lavender/ blue highlights*
D) ●   *Transparent dark green*

Notes

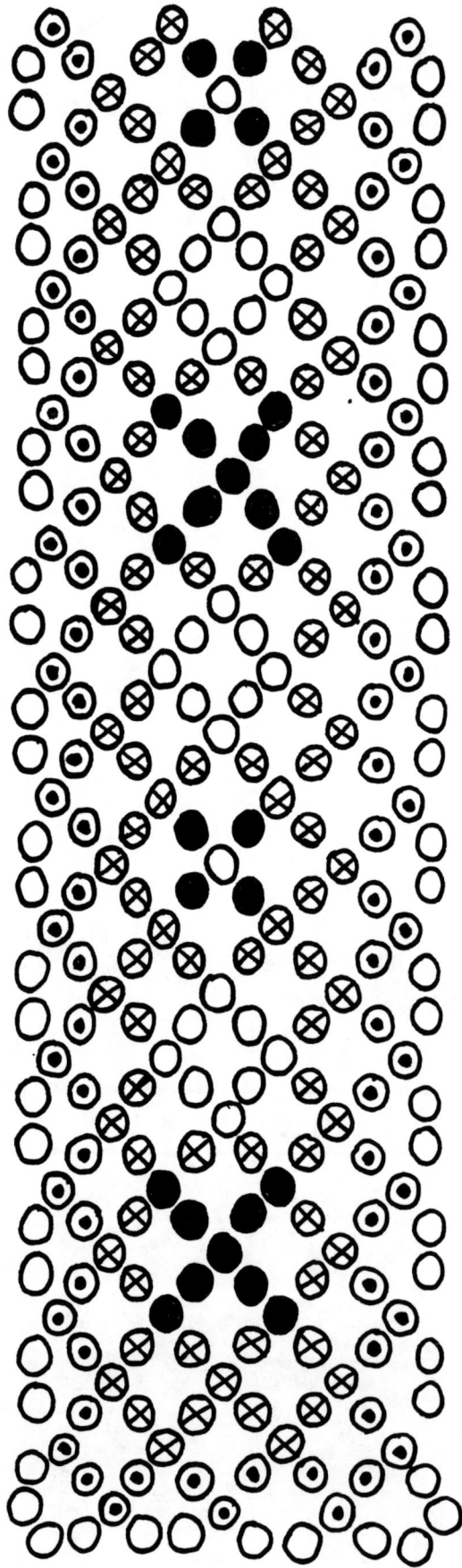

I

Color Selections for Bracelet I

1.

A) ○   *Pearl white*

B) ⊙   *Bronze*

C) ✪   *White*

2.

A) ○   *Pink*

B) ⊙   *White*

C) ✪   *Transparent olive green*

3.

A) ○   *Matte blue*

B) ⊙   *Dark blue*

C) ✪   *Transparent blue*

Notes

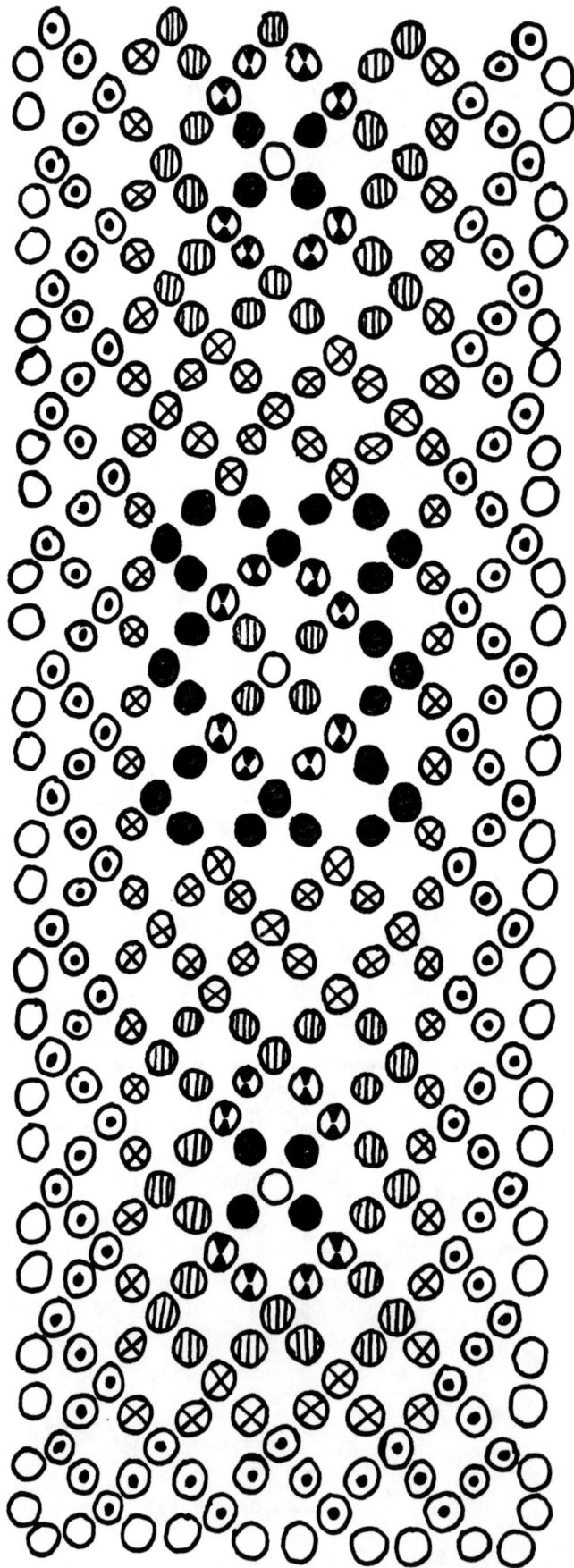

J

Color Selections for Bracelet J

1.

A)   ○   *Transparent pink/ gold highlights*
B)   ⊙   *Pearl white*
C)   ✹   *Transparent/ rainbow*
D)   ◍   *Red*
E)   ✪   *Pink*
F)   ⬤   *Transparent brown*

2.

A)   ○   *Transparent turquoise/ gold highlights*
B)   ⊙   *Pearl white*
C)   ✹   *Transparent coffee*
D)   ◍   *Transparent dark brown*
E)   ✪   *Turquoise*
F)   ⬤   *Transparent blue*

3.

A)   ○   *Black*
B)   ⊙   *Transparent light gray*
C)   ✹   *Burgundy red*
D)   ◍   *Black*
E)   ✪   *Metallic black*
F)   ⬤   *Pearl coffee*

Notes

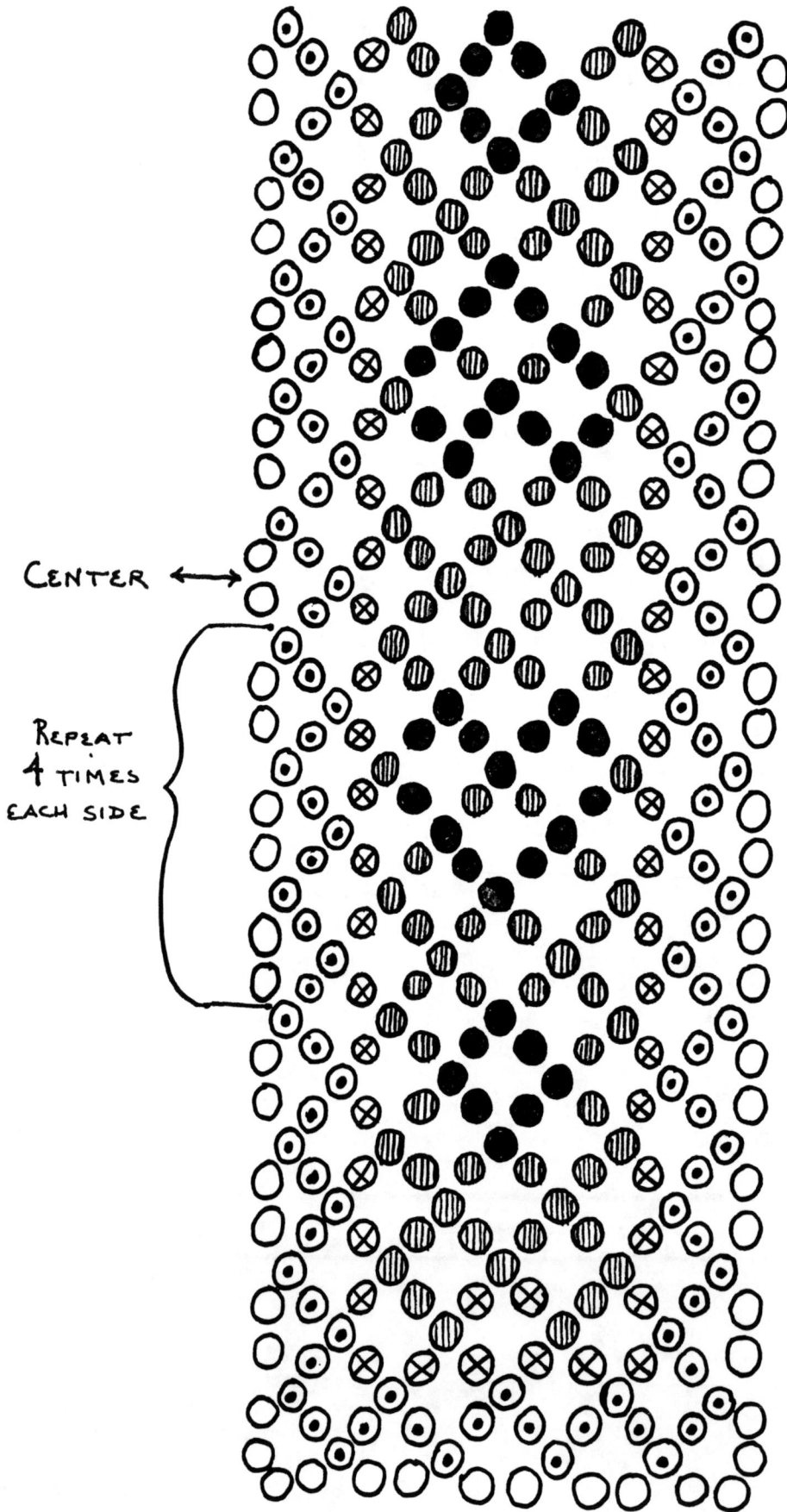

K

Center ←→

Repeat
4 times
each side

Color Selections for Bracelet K

1.

A)	○	*Pearl light sea-green*
B)	⊙	*Pearl white*
C)	✪	*Pearl sea-green*
D)	◍	*Pale pearl sea-green*
E)	●	*Pearl sea-green*

2.

A)	○	*Red*
B)	⊙	*Pearl white*
C)	✪	*Red*
D)	◍	*White*
E)	●	*Red*

3.

A)	○	*Transparent dark green*
B)	⊙	*Transparent pink/ gold highlights*
C)	✪	*Matte dark purple*
D)	◍	*Transparent light purple*
E)	●	*Matte dark purple*

Notes

47

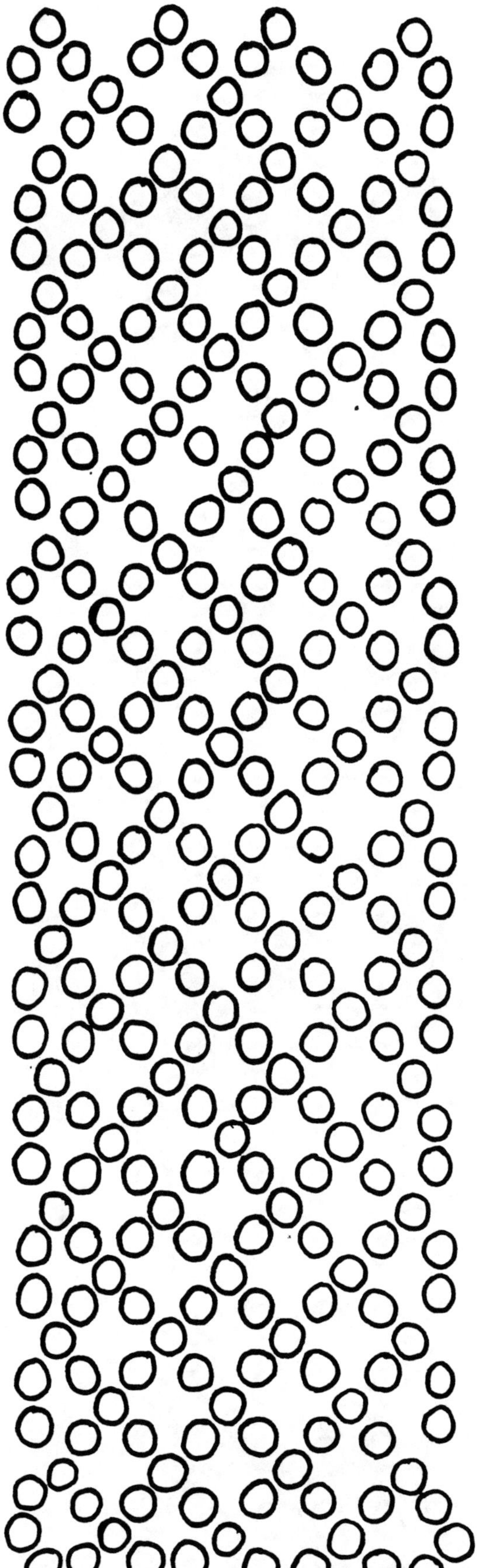

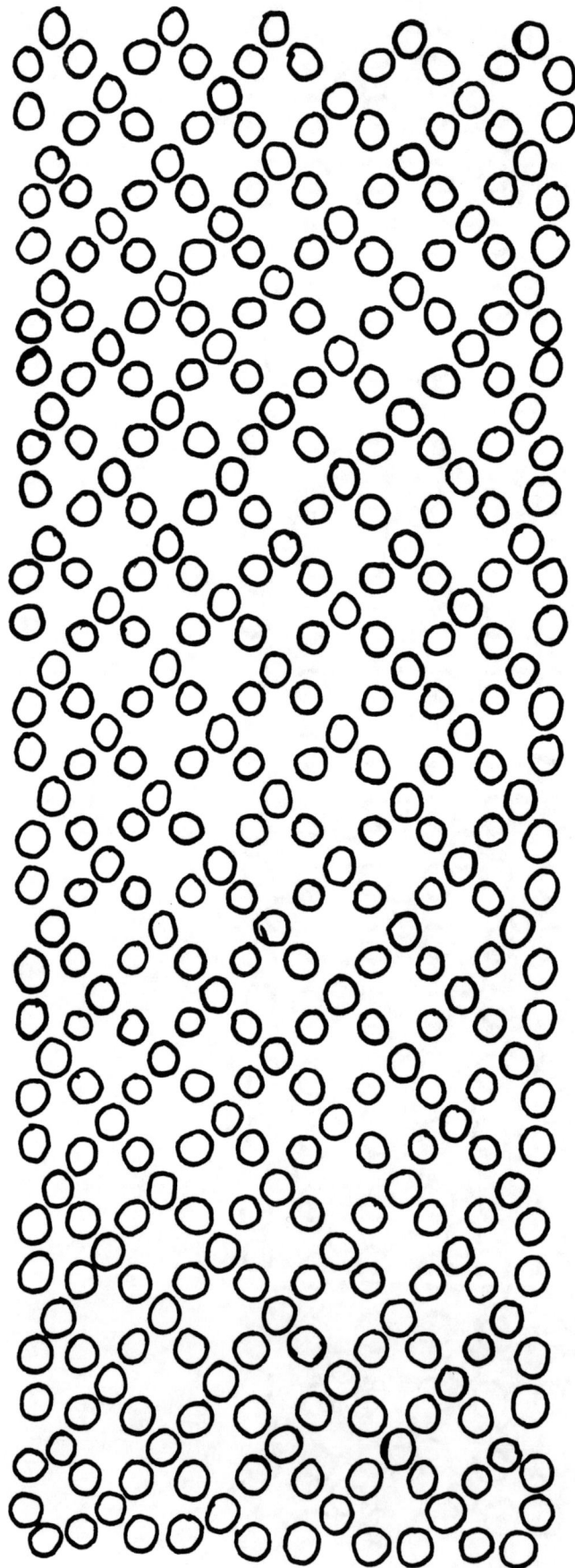

Suppliers

Fire Mountain Gems
28195 Redwood Hwy.
Cave Junction, OR 97523-9304
Phone (800) 423-2319
Fax (541) 592-3103

Baker Bay Bead Co.
35655 Shoreview, Drive
Dorena, OR 97434
Phone (541) 942-3941
Fax (541) 942-8479

The Bead Shop
899 South Coast Highway
Laguna Beach, CA 92651
Phone (714) 494-2115
Fax (714) 494-0380